Victory
Over a Critical
Spirit

Jim Hammer

TEACH Services, Inc.
P U B L I S H I N G
www.TEACHServices.com

Copyright © 2013 TEACH Services, Inc.
ISBN-13: 978-1-4796-0010-6 (Paperback)
ISBN-13: 978-1-4796-0043-4 (Saddle Stitch)
ISBN-13: 978-1-4796-0011-3 (Epub)
ISBN-13: 978-1-4796-0012-0 (Kindle/Mobi)

Published by
TEACH Services, Inc.
P U B L I S H I N G
www.TEACHServices.com

Dedication

To my wife, Joanne, who has been so loving,
compassionate, and forgiving.

Thank You

To all who encouraged me during the writing
of this book—especially June Strong.

Introduction

You may be wondering why I wrote a book on criticism. Isn't the book itself a critical statement? As you read I hope you will realize that I have taken great effort to focus on victory over a critical attitude and not to focus on the criticizer. As a Christian for the past thirty years, I have experienced within the church family inconsistencies in the Christlike spirit that the Bible teaches us to model. It appears to go from an ultra-conservative extreme to a very liberal extreme.

In both camps there seems to be an attitude that "we are right" and everyone else has to measure up to our standard and ideas. Although we believe we are doing God's will, our spirit is far from that of Christ's.

In doing research for this project, I soon realized that this critical spirit has permeated all churches and all denominations. Church families are being torn apart, the work of God is being hindered, and the enemy is rejoicing. However, God has His people in every church, and they are striving to be more and more like Jesus. Praise God!

Chapter 1

When and Where This Critical Spirit Started

There is a critical spirit, disguised as the spirit of Jesus, that has infiltrated the church family. Revelation 12:17 states that the devil is making war with God's church and His people, and the enemy of our souls is using those who are, or who profess to be, followers of Jesus to fight against each other. It is time to wake up from the slumber that so easily besets us. When I mentioned to one friend of mine that I was writing a book about criticism in the church, he said, "We don't need that—we already know how to criticize." Although he was being humorous, his thought was right on. There is a critical element in all of us that sprung to life in the Garden of Eden when Adam accepted the enemy's character. The enemy then separated Adam and Eve from God and then from each other.

Criticism started in heaven when Lucifer questioned the authority of God. One third of the heavenly angels agreed with him and were cast out of heaven. Sometime later Satan then made his way to the Garden of Eden. The enemy questioned God's word and planted a negative seed of doubt and criticism in Eve's mind, and a short time later, after Eve disobeyed and was caught, she criticized the serpent. Then Adam was critical of God and the woman He gave him (Gen. 3:12). But notice that God did not criticize anyone.

We inherited this same type of negative attitude, even to the extent that we think it is normal to find fault with one another. And unless we cultivate a positive attitude, the enemy will have gained the victory over us. *The attitude we display is an attitude we choose.* We can have a positive or a negative attitude; it's our decision.

Our victory is in Jesus Christ. He promised in Genesis 3:15 to put hatred between the enemy and God's people. It is not our natural tendency to hate evil, but it's a supernatural tendency instilled in us through the Holy Spirit. I have confidence that all of heaven is doing everything that can be done to save us. God is longsuffering with us, not willing that any should perish (2 Peter 3:9).

I've heard the terminology "we, they, us, and them" used when a person is criticizing another person or group of people. This only separates us more. So often you will hear a church member say, "One part of the church family thinks this or that, and the other part of the family has a different opinion." Aren't we all one family? Isn't it time we realize it? It's too late in earth's history to conduct ourselves in a way that is not in harmony with Jesus.

Why this critical spirit? How can it be avoided? Where can one go for assistance? When will these extreme attitudes or polarizations cease?

I pray that the following chapters will be a blessing for you and that your relationship with Jesus, your family, your church family, and your community will be eternally enhanced.

Chapter 2

My Own Self-Righteousness

If this message doesn't have a strong foundation, it will not stand. So I would like to lay a foundation as to why I am writing about this subject.

For many years I had a very judgmental spirit. Unbeknownst to me, this critical spirit was killing my church family. Most of all, it was killing me spiritually. My "first love" had become almost nonexistent. But praise the Lord, He did not leave me in that condition. As I look back on those days, I'm ashamed of the way I conducted myself. I set out as an ambassador for Jesus, but almost immediately my judgmental spirit was evident.

Shortly after the Holy Spirit touched my life, I had to travel into the city of Buffalo, New York, for an appointment. When I got out of my vehicle, a homeless person asked me for a dollar. I just "knew" he was going to buy alcohol with it, so I said, "I won't give you any money, but I do have something for you," and I gave him a piece of Christian literature.

He remarked, "Oh, you're a Christian. What does John 3:16 say?"

"I don't know," I admitted.

He recited it! Then he asked, "What is the shortest verse in the Bible?"

I again responded, "I don't know."

He told me that scripture too. We talked for about thirty minutes, and yes, I gave him a dollar. Whenever I went to Buffalo, I would look for Bob so that we could have lunch together.

Some years later I picked up a morning newspaper and to my surprise saw Bob's picture on the front page. Reading the article, I discovered that my friend was a true Christian in a very practical way. He lived at the City Mission, and when someone would come in and there was no room for him, Bob would give him his bed. He would also panhandle money for those who were less fortunate than himself. I read the article in disbelief. My friend never once mentioned this aspect of his life—he just humbly did it.

Initially I had judged Bob as a homeless alcoholic with no sense of purpose in his life. I was looking at him through a critical eye. The Lord, however, had a divine plan for that appointment. The Lord wanted to reveal to me a glimpse of my own character.

Jesus knew my character, and right from the beginning He was trying to guide my thoughts, but as time went on I became more and more critical. I believed I was doing the will of Jesus, never realizing that the enemy was behind a lot of my words and actions. I thank God for how mercifully He dealt with me when in reality I was not very compassionate or patient with others, especially within my church family.

When I became a Christian and joined a Bible-believing church, my desire was to follow Jesus to the best of my ability. I knew then and still know now that the Holy Spirit led me to this church. However, it wasn't long before I became works-oriented. I felt compelled to do something, so I got involved in everything possible, but I also believed everything had to be done precisely the way I wanted it. If it wasn't done my way, then it couldn't possibly be correct. I even remarked to one pastor, "I don't think anyone can do things as well as I can." How absurd!

But to this precious pastor's credit—because he didn't want to crush my spirit—he simply stated, "I'm glad you have so much confidence in yourself." I really had a high opinion of myself and the capabilities I possessed. Eventually I was nicknamed "the Pope," and being a former Catholic, I thought that was some kind of honor.

I judged others by my standards, and I tried to make them a carbon copy of myself. If they didn't dress, talk, or eat right, if they wore jewelry or if their attitude wasn't like mine, then their relationship with Jesus wasn't genuine. I tried to make everyone into my image. Jesus surely didn't need anymore like me!

It is God's purpose to recreate us once again into His image, but I was, sadly, blind to that fact. We must pattern our life after Jesus. No human being is to replace Jesus in our life. Many think highly of their own opinion, but Paul states that we should esteem others as better than ourselves (Phil. 2:3). Oh what a fantastic experience we would all have if everyone could have this mindset. God's Word says that this is attainable: "Let this mind be in you which was also in Christ Jesus" (verse 5).

God has given us the privilege of working with Him, so let's not squander the opportunities that Jesus places before us. He desires to pour out His blessings on us. But we must seek the opportunities that God has planned for us to minister to others, for the purpose of allowing the blessings to flow through us to others. The Lord places many opportunities before us—take advantage of them; they are usually a once in a lifetime experience.

And remember this eye-opening statement: The "I" problem is sin. When you take the "I" out of sin, there is no sin!

Chapter 3

First Life-Changing Experience

Eventually three life-changing experiences occurred to me. When my youngest daughter was fifteen or sixteen years old, she got into everything. Cigarettes, alcohol, and drugs became the norm. Some nights she didn't come home. When she did, one argument led to another one. As a father who loved his daughter very much, I was frustrated. We would argue about who she was with, what she was doing, and where she was going. At times I would even check her eyes to see if they were dilated, knowing it was useless to talk to her if she was high on drugs.

Finally, the Holy Spirit impressed upon me that I was not conducting myself as a Christian. Not only that, I was convicted that I was a stumbling block to my daughter. I fell to my knees and confessed my failure as a father and asked for forgiveness from my heavenly Father. Then I placed her into His hands, knowing that He was a more superior Father than I could ever be. I actually felt the burden of responsibility for my daughter lifted from my shoulders when I poured out my heart in prayer. The Lord had taken my problem, and He gave me the peace of mind that only comes from surrender.

I was also impressed with the fact that ever since sin entered this world we have all come from, and are in, dysfunctional families. Through much prayer, I allowed the Lord to change me, and then I watched as He also changed my daughter. Over a period of six months or so, I began to see a change in my daughter's attitude. She started coming home at night; eventually there was no more smoking, drinking, or drugs. It was a time of praise and rejoicing before the Lord. About six months later she was baptized. I then realized that with me in the way the Holy Spirit couldn't do what He does best, bring souls into a saving, lasting, loving relationship with Jesus.

It is imperative that we allow the Holy Spirit the freedom to impress upon others the same saving influences that He used to bring us to Jesus. I believe the most influential thing we can do is to live the life that Jesus wants us to live. That will be more powerful than any sermon that is preached in any church. Also, I do believe that we really do not understand the power of prayer.

But my spiritual journey was far from done. What happened a few years later really stunned me.

Chapter 4

Questioning My Own Spiritual Condition

The second event, which happened a few years later, occurred while involved in a van ministry in New York City. My family and I were invited to volunteer at this ministry, and we got excited and decided to assist in whatever way we could. At that time I didn't know that the Lord would use it to prompt me to make a radical change in my way of thinking. Because I still had the attitude of wanting to do things my way, the Lord placed the leadership role of this ministry in the hands of someone else. It was a person whom I admired and respected; thus, it was rather easy to follow directions and do what I was asked to do without imposing upon her the way I thought everything should be done.

After volunteering for a number of years, we were invited to a wedding that took place at the ministry headquarters. It was a very proper Christian wedding. The men wore suits; the women wore dresses. The music was appropriate, and everything was going well. However, as the ceremony was about to begin, I looked around and, to my surprise, noticed a young lady who had just arrived wearing makeup, jeans, a blouse, and a denim vest. I could not believe what I was seeing. Did my eyes betray me? No, she was at this wedding dressed inappropriately. Right away I knew she was in need of spiritual enlightenment, and I took it upon myself to put her on the right path.

At the reception I eventually made my way over to her and started some small talk with the ulterior motive of setting her on the right track. Eventually I asked her if she was a Christian. She replied in the affirmative and said that she had just been baptized last week. Naturally I assumed that she belonged to a very charismatic movement, so I asked her what church she attended. To my dismay, it was the same denomination of which I was a member. To say I was shocked would be an understatement. I asked her who baptized her. I knew the pastor she named, and it just didn't sound like him.

Sometime later I had the opportunity to speak with this pastor, and I asked him why he had decided to baptize her. He said, "Well, she was under conviction by the Holy Spirit to be baptized." He had called the conference president and was told that "if she is under conviction, then you baptize her." I had known both of these men for a while, and I knew they were servants of God. Although I was still concerned, I thought, *Who am I to question the work of the Holy Spirit and the servants whom He is working through?*

The biggest shock was yet to come. I asked her if she would like to volunteer at the ministry, and she agreed. I then mentioned that she would have to wear a skirt and blouse or a dress. She quickly stated that she could do that, but she informed me that she would need a ride. I agreed to provide transportation for her the next morning.

As someone used to living in a small country town, I now found myself trying to navigate through New York City. Wanting to be on time, I had left early and was able to find the house. While we were driving back to the ministry headquarters, I asked her how she became a Christian. The Holy Spirit did not prepare me for the testimony I was about to hear, and it hit me like a ton of rocks.

She was living on the streets of New York City when the Lord touched her life. She had been homeless and was using heavy drugs, smoking, drinking and living a life that wasn't in harmony with Jesus. When Jesus touched her life, things started changing. Cigarettes and alcohol fell by the wayside. The Holy Spirit was moving on her heart, and she was responding. Praise God! When she stopped using drugs, her boyfriend rejected and abandoned her.

She said, "I cried and cried, but then I realized I had Someone better—I had Jesus!" That's when the Holy Spirit strongly convicted me of the fact that this precious child of God, who the day before I had judged as being in need of spiritual enlightenment, had a better relationship with Jesus than I did. At that very moment my attitude started to change. I began looking at others through the eyes of Jesus and seeing who they could be through His power and strength—"'Not by might nor by power, but by My Spirit,' says the Lord of hosts" (Zech. 4:6).

Each one of us is in need of life-changing experiences that will open our eyes and allow Jesus to make us into the person He wants us to be. Jesus will give us opportunity after opportunity to change, but this can only happen as we allow the Holy Spirit to show us our own hearts, thereby focusing on Jesus and taking our eyes and minds off of each other. By beholding Jesus we will become like Him.

If you want to look for the negative, you'll find enough to criticize, but if you desire to be a positive-thinking person, you will be led to see people and situations in a different light. You will be led to see them as Jesus sees them. This experience helped me to realize that my whole attitude needed to be adjusted. Consequently, because of this realization, I was now more open to the Holy Spirit's leading.

We waste so much time, both ours and His, by being so hardheaded and stiff-necked! We are such slow learners! I'm glad that God has an abundant amount of patience. His mercy should overwhelm us, yet we are so impatient with one another. Impatient! Yes, we want everything done yesterday. Sad, isn't it? If we want this to change, we have to change, not someone else.

Chapter 5

Another Holy Spirit Intervention

The third experience happened a few years later as the Holy Spirit was drawing my son to Jesus. He was living with his girlfriend and their son when he started to respond to the promptings of the Holy Spirit. He called me week after week to talk. Finally he called and said that he was going to attend church. My first impulse was to say, "What about the way you are living?" But the Holy Spirit whispered in my ear, "Be still." The following week when he called he mentioned that he had joined the personal ministry team, and again I wanted to say, "What about the way you are living?" Once again, the Holy Spirit said, "Keep quiet."

The following week he progressed to going door to door to hand out literature. You probably know by now what I wanted to say to him, but I didn't. When he called me the fourth week and told me he was going to give Bible studies, I could barely contain myself. Virtually sitting on the edge of my chair, I felt compelled to discuss with him about the way he was living. Yet the Holy Spirit really impressed me to "KEEP QUIET," and I am glad I did.

I had often uplifted my son and his girlfriend in prayer, and I doubled my efforts. I realized that this situation was in the Lord's hands, the best place for it to be. On week five, right on schedule, I received his usual call. But this time he informed me that he and his girlfriend had decided to get married. I almost jumped out of my chair. "Praise God!" I declared. I then realized that in all our prior conversations, if I hadn't listened to the Holy Spirit and instead told my son what I was thinking, they might have gotten married for me. But now I knew they were getting married for Jesus.

Isn't that the way it should be? We need to get out of the Holy Spirit's way, yet many of us try to usurp the authority of the Holy Spirit. As parents, because we want the best for our children, we make the fatal mistake of trying too hard. Instead of leading them to Jesus, we become stumbling blocks, and we drive them away from the very One who can save them.

My son is now an ordained elder in the church. He gives Bible studies to the youth in his neighborhood, and he travels to various churches to preach. He and his wife have four sons, and their children are active in church and a blessing in their community. The oldest son is now in college, and the others will be following him soon.

This is just one example of what the Holy Spirit can do if we allow Him. All of this could have been destroyed if I had decided to follow my own desires and expressed my critical thoughts to my son; thus taking control and not allowing the Holy Spirit to work in their lives. We serve such an awesome Creator!

Chapter 6

One Pastor's Influence

I want to share with you the story of one pastor. He is the humblest pastor I have ever had the privilege of working with. I was the head elder at the time, and we immediately bonded. When he first arrived, we talked for about forty-five minutes in the church office. We laughed, cried, and prayed together.

Before delivering his first sermon, this new pastor called a meeting with the church membership at large. He wanted to know just what we expected from him. Now let me mention that this church family was evenly divided into two groups. One part of the family wanted to hear our church doctrine preached; the other wanted to hear more about Jesus as the center of everything the church teaches. But instead we were criticizing each other for these varying viewpoints.

When the meeting started, the first group talked about how beautiful our doctrines are and that we needed to hear more of them. This thought was expressed again and again with more and more determination. I found myself wanting to speak a word regarding Jesus being the center of our beliefs, but I was impressed to say nothing.

After listening patiently for about thirty minutes, the pastor spoke, and all eyes looked intently at him. "Our doctrine is beautiful. So you want me to preach smooth teachings, things that will tickle your ears."

I thought, *What is this guy talking about?*"

But he then added, "I could speak on what happens to us when we die, and when you leave, you can say, 'I already knew that.' So you see, that would be a smooth teaching, a teaching that would tickle your ears. Anything you already know becomes a smooth teaching."

I had never thought of anything like that before. Then he went on to say, "Jesus longs for your heart, and when He has your heart, everything else will fall into place."

At this I realized that this pastor was just the man the Lord knew we needed. The Christlike spirit of that church started to develop immediately, and the Lord started sending former members and new visitors to our church each Sabbath. This pastor was with us for two years, and our attendance more than tripled within that time period.

Of course, we were overjoyed because many souls were being won for the Lord, the church was filling up, and we also realized that the Lord could trust us with His people. God has so many of His people, unchurched or in other churches, just waiting for us to get our act together so He can send them to us.

About a year after this experience, this same pastor was conducting a board meeting in which some of the board members were criticizing and accusing him about an incident of which I knew he had no knowledge of. He listened very patiently, as always. After fifteen minutes or so of accusatory comments, he humbly said, "I'm so sorry. Please forgive me." With that answer, the meeting changed from being hostile to being centered on Christ. He never once tried to defend himself, which is our natural human tendency. Needless to say, his reply was an outstanding educational moment for me. We have since moved to different areas, but we have still maintained our friendship through the years.

Chapter 7

Experience as a Lay Pastor

After some years I was asked to be the lay pastor of one of our sister churches. The congregation was renting a church from another denomination. We started out with about twelve members. The Spirit was present, and within six months the church had forty-five to fifty people in attendance. Prayer meetings were well attended; business meetings were relaxed and productive; and we all looked forward to worship services. Furthermore, a twenty-four hour low-power radio station was to be a reality in the near future. Everything was moving along smoothly, and it wasn't long before we decided to build our own church.

Things started out very well, but it soon became evident that the beautiful spirit we once had was rapidly deteriorating. After looking at thirty-five pieces of property, some with buildings on them and some just vacant acreage, the church family was fracturing. When a property was presented, half of the church family would approve and the other half would oppose. It didn't matter which part of the church family approved, the other part disapproved. The more we discussed different pieces of property, the more divisive we became. This went on for about two years. We were hopelessly self-destructing; and a critical spirit developed. We were finding fault with everything, no matter how innocent or good it was. Members were on the phone discussing different issues, and all the ministries of the church were being undermined by it.

After months of ill feelings, months of meeting together, we were polarized more than ever. Our conference president, bless his heart, held meetings with us week after week—six meetings within two months—but to no avail. Serious accusations flew in both directions. We were too stiff-necked, stubborn, proud, and critical to allow the Holy Spirit to change us. By this time the radio station was about to become a reality, and the church family was in complete disarray. I think you get the picture. What started out as a positive experience had now rapidly declined into a frustrating and negative journey.

Remember this, the Holy Spirit is always, and I emphasize always, trying to show us our faults, not the faults of someone else. We have enough to deal with as we search our own hearts. As the problems at church increased, I started to search my own heart; I was not naïve enough to believe that I was not part of the problem. Consequently, what the Holy Spirit revealed to me wasn't a pretty picture. He impressed me with the fact that I was not representing Jesus the way He wanted me to. There was much to repent of.

My prayer life went into high gear. I was very specific. I prayed like this: "Father, whoever is hindering Your work, move them out of the way. If You have to, put them to sleep, but save them." I didn't pray this out of any type of maliciousness, but out of concern for the Lord's work and concern for their salvation. Then I added, "And Father, if I am hindering Your work, move me out of Your way. If You have to, put me to sleep, but save me. Amen." Within three months the Lord moved some of the church family to other locations. I don't want to elaborate any further on this matter for fear of opening up old wounds, but this situation proved that God desires to help His children come together in unity when they turn to Him.

When I look at the major cause of most church problems, I believe it is rooted in the critical spirit, and this spirit is rooted in pride—the pride of exalting oneself, thinking oneself superior to someone else, or acting that his/her opinion is the one that needs to be followed. When you take the "I" out of pride, there is no pride. The critical spirit may start out as a bud, but it won't take long before it is in full bloom.

I've discovered that most of the focal points of contention in church are centered around food, dress, theology, music, jewelry, and money. Although these issues are important, they cannot take the place of the gospel. If the critical spirit is not brought under the influence of the Holy Spirit, every ministry will be hindered and undermined by it. And it will be virtually impossible for the Lord to open the church doors to those that are on the fringe just waiting to be brought into the fold. When we have the wrong spirit, God cannot trust us with His people. It is time to realize the wretchedness of our spiritual condition and go forward into the Lord's ripened vineyard. Jesus will give us the spirit and courage and also supply our every need. The work is the Lord's and He has all the resources of heaven at His disposal.

The Father, Son, and Holy Spirit are not caught off guard by the enemy's attempt to disrupt the church. They are prepared for any attempt on his part to create havoc among us. Do we trust Them enough to get us through any situation that arises? Our words may say that we trust God to take care of our church, but our actions speak otherwise when we attack each other.

As we encounter different personalities in our home, community, and church, and we speak critical words and entertain critical thoughts, do we really believe that when Jesus returns we will walk right into eternity with Him? We are perfecting our characters here on earth in preparation for heaven.

I understand that some people are extremely challenging to deal with, but if we are to be like Christ, we have to learn how to live and work with difficult people. One thing I do when someone irritates me is pray that they will be my neighbor in heaven. You can't be upset with someone you're praying for.

When we look at Scripture and read about the spiritual giants such as Abraham, Joseph, Moses, Joshua, David, Daniel, and all the apostles, including Paul, we should realize that they would count it a privilege to be alive now. They could do a much better job of ushering in the second coming of Jesus than we could, yet God has chosen you and me to be alive now at this exciting time of earth's history. We have been given the awesome privilege of being here as a witness for Jesus to the world. Are you being a good witness? Are you representing Jesus' character, our Creator and Restorer, or are you acting like the enemy who wants to destroy us? It's your choice. The spirit of Jesus is "love, joy, peace, longsuffering, kindness, goodness, faithfulness, gentleness, [and] self-control" (Gal. 5:22, 23). Jesus' ministry revolved around uplifting and encouraging people. The enemy is just the opposite. Satan wants to discourage us, knock us down, criticize our actions, and most of all steal our joy and eventually destroy us. The only safety we have is in Jesus!

This statement is very timely: "The time has come for a thorough reformation to take place. When this reformation begins, the spirit of prayer will actuate every believer and will banish from the church the spirit of discord and strife" (*Testimonies for the Church*, vol. 8, p. 251).

As our church started on the upward path again, the Lord impressed me that I needed to step back from my pastoral position. I followed His guidance. The Lord sent us just the right person as a pastor, and we were grateful for that. We started praying for each other;

we started communicating with each other again and loving each other once more. We also voted in a church policy that stated that we would not listen to criticism or promote a negative spirit. I was asked, "How do you implement that?" It's simple; you just don't respond to any negative, criticizing remarks and the negative, criticizing spirit dies.

It wasn't long before the Lord started sending His people to us. We realized that the Lord now knew it was safe to lead His people to us. The Lord knew that we would love them into His special end-time, Christ-centered message.

What about our children? Does our critical spirit affect them? Read on!

Chapter 8

How Does This Affect Our Children?

A great danger with negativity is that we pass on our critical spirit to our children. If we have a critical spirit, we naturally express it in our homes, and our children are exposed to it. Thus, they come to believe that this is the normal way of life. At mealtime we will sit around the table and criticize anyone who isn't in agreement with us. We talk about them and try to make ourselves look good. Our pastors and teachers are usually the ones we criticize the most—and isn't that the way the enemy wants it? Although we may not invite them to dinner, they become our main course of discussion.

Lord, have mercy on us! If only we could get a glimpse of how Jesus sees us—how He looks into the depths of our being and sees us for who and what we really are—we would, no doubt, cry out, "Oh, what a wretched person I am!" There is no doubt in my mind that the Holy Spirit is trying to show each of us who we really are.

Our children, although they may seem preoccupied, take it all in. When we're on the telephone making negative comments and gossiping, the children are absorbing everything, and worst of all, they're only hearing one side of the conversation. We do our children such a disservice. As parents we are supposed to be preparing them for eternity with Jesus, and yet we oftentimes have the attitude of the enemy. The Word of God states, "If you bite and devour one another, beware lest you are consumed by one another" (Gal. 5:15).

If we are truly God's children, then we are told to "love one another as Jesus loves us; then everyone will know that you are My disciples" (see John 13:35). If we followed Jesus' command, we would protect one another's reputation instead of trying to destroy it. Read all of Galatians chapter 5. You'll see in verses 19 through 23 that Paul mentions the works of the flesh. Among them are some serious sins: hatred, contention, jealousy, outbursts of wrath, selfish ambitions, and dissension. Paul goes on to state that "those who practice such things will not inherit the kingdom of God" (verse 21).

Paul doesn't leave us in discouragement; he then goes on to give the fruits of the Spirit: "love, joy, peace, longsuffering, kindness, goodness, faithfulness, gentleness [or humility, and] self-control" (verses 22, 23). He then states, "Against such there is no law" (verse 23). We can have as much of these as we want. Philippians 4:13 says, "I can do all things through Christ who strengthens me." So you can either have the lust of the flesh or you can have the fruits of the Spirit. The enemy can't force you to sin, and Jesus will not force you to follow Him. It is an individual decision. We need to exemplify loving, compassionate, and positive attitudes to our children. And we have the same responsibility to the children in the church family.

We either spread the love of God or the hatred of the enemy. It is our decision. What choice are you going to make, and how will you accomplish it? Can there be victory over such rebellion against God and against our neighbor? Yes! The victory can be ours if we allow the Holy Spirit to mold and shape us into the likeness of Jesus. Read the Word of God. Consume it. Seek forgiveness from God and your neighbor. Claim the promise in 1 John 1:9 to be "cleansed of all unrighteousness" and let "God's righteousness flow through you" (see Isa. 54:17). Pray like you have never prayed before to be like Jesus. If you made any critical comments in front of your children, take them with you when you apologize, or else they will still have the same opinion of that person because of the negative statements you made. In the Lord's Prayer of Matthew 6, the only part that Jesus re-emphasized was that of forgiveness (see verses 14, 15).

See how many days you can go without making one critical comment in your home. At first you might not be able to make it through one hour, but continue to present it before the throne of grace, and God will give you the victory over a critical spirit. However, be prepared because the enemy will do everything possible to have you represent him and his attitude to those around you.

If we are like Christ, we will draw other people to us, including our children. We wonder why our children are leaving the church. Could it be because of the criticism and gossip? They hear us make negative comments about someone and then they see us greet that same person as if they were our long-lost friend.

During one of our heated board meetings, unbeknownst to us, one of my sons (who was eleven at the time) and another young boy were sitting in the stairway. As the meeting progressed and we became more argumentative and critical, the boy turned to my son and said,

"Nice church, huh?" When my son repeated that to me it left a lasting impression.

There was one dear sister in our church family who, no matter what I said, always presented the opposite view. This went on for a number of years, and our relationship was strained at best. One day when I was driving down the road and thinking about this woman, the Holy Spirit impressed me that she only had my best interest at heart and was concerned about my salvation. That was an eye-opener for me. From that day to this, I have looked at her in a totally different way. It didn't take long before we became friends.

As Christians we are called to encourage and uplift one another. It all depends on how we look at a person or any given situation. Do we look at others through the eyes of Jesus or the eyes of the enemy?

Chapter 9

Oh That We Would be Like Jesus

Many people bring up the fact that Jesus was critical. They cite the many instances He rebuked the religious leaders, drove the moneychangers from the temple, etc. Please keep in mind that this was at the end of His ministry. Critical people seem to forget about the entire life of Jesus. Only the so-called critical moments at the end of His life are remembered. Also, Jesus didn't criticize like we do. He did so with a breaking heart, and He could also read the hearts of His persecutors—we cannot. Also, remember this most important fact, Jesus was preparing to shed His blood for them, even to give up heaven itself for the entire human race. Are you ready to die for the person you are criticizing?

The religious leaders, God's own people, brought Jesus to the judgment hall of Pilate. They wanted Jesus crucified. They would not be satisfied until He was dead. The heathen governor on more than one occasion stated, "I find no fault in Him at all." Amazing that the condemnation came from within the church and the encouragement came from without. We receive enough criticism from our families, our fellow employees, and other Christians who don't understand some of our decisions. We don't need any faultfinding from within our church family. We are called to encourage and uplift each other. Please don't misunderstand this; known sin within the church needs to be addressed, but only in the same way that Jesus dealt with it. His burdened heart went out to the sinner while He hated the sin.

Jesus was surrounded by sin and evil His entire life on this sin-sick planet. However, He was filled with the love, sympathy and compassion from on high. *The Desire of Ages* says, "Every pang that rent His heart, every insult that was heaped upon His head ... was open to His view before He laid aside His crown and royal robe, and stepped down from the throne, to clothe His divinity with humanity. The path from the manger to Calvary was all before His eyes.... He knew it all, and yet He said,'"Lo, I come"' (p. 410).

Jesus was inconvenienced every step of the way, yet He kept His focus on the mission before Him. Jesus is the Light of the world and we are to let His love and light flow through us to others, and yes, many times we too will be inconvenienced. Yet isn't it exciting to have the privilege of being Christ's ambassadors to the world? The King of all creation has chosen us to be His ambassadors. Amazing grace!

We have to represent Jesus every step of the way. When I look at the church structure, starting with the membership and then the local church officers, elders, pastors, and conference officers, I expect each group to be spiritually above the previous group. For example, the local church leaders should be spiritually above the membership; pastors should be spiritually above the local leaders; and the conference officers should be a cut above the pastors, and so on.

There has to be harmony in every leadership group, if disharmony exists in any area, it will also be experienced by the group they are supposed to be ministering too, and every ministry will be affected either positively or negatively. This depends on the harmony and attitude of the leadership. If we are divided in any group area, the entire church family will suffer.

Chapter 10

Is the Health Message the Gospel?

First let me state that before I became a Christian, I started researching secular material on sickness and disease. The more I read the more I realized "we are what we eat." I started eliminating flesh foods from my diet. I don't recall what I read about pork but that was the first animal I stopped consuming. The more I read these articles, the more meat I eliminated from my diet. Eventually I became a vegetarian, and I'm glad I did.

Six years later I started reading the Bible and noticed that the secular material I had read corresponded with the religious material I was now studying. I realized that the Lord had been leading me years before I even opened a Bible. As a matter of fact, when I was first invited to church and was told there would be a fellowship dinner, I thought the folks would think I was a little strange since I didn't smoke, drink alcohol, or eat meat. Naturally I was surprised when the meal started and I discovered that this group of people believed and practiced as I did. Then I knew for sure that the Lord had been leading me through the years.

Now my meal preference is a vegan diet. However, let me share what has taken place over the past three decades. Many of the church folks who are so involved in the health message put that message in front of everything else. This happens many times to the point that it becomes the gospel and everything revolves around the health message. For example, one person I've known for thirty years even judged ministers by what they ate. These folks have an extremely critical spirit, and if you try to defend the object of their criticism, their retort is something about what that person eats. I refer to them as "kitchen police."

The following story illustrates how this critical nature hurts others. My nephew was baptized in the ocean at Virginia Beach. His wife invited their neighbor to whom they had been witnessing to for a few years. After the baptism we all gathered in a large tent that had been erected on the beach for a fellowship dinner. When I was ready to eat, I noticed that my nephew's neighbor was not there. I inquired as to her whereabouts and was informed that she had gone home. I knew she had planned to stay and eat because she had brought a dish to contribute to the meal. Further investigation revealed that she had prepared a dish of beans with bacon on top. Because of unkind comments about it, she took it and left in tears. The next day I visited her home and apologized. She was very gracious, but I knew the damage was already done. Once again, because of food, someone had been chased away. What a shame that we are so insensitive to God's fragile children! "Do not destroy with your food the one for whom Christ died. Therefore do not let your good be spoken of as evil" (Rom. 14:15, 16).

In interviewing many pastors and church leaders about the most common problems within the church, I found that all of them said it centered on the priority of the health message. In some cases it was even dividing the church family. They said—and I agree—that a person becomes unbalanced when going to extremes with the health message. What do I mean by too extreme? It is when the health message replaces the gospel.

Barnabas' real name was Joses (or Joseph), but he was renamed Barnabas, which is translated "son of encouragement" (Acts 4:36). Oh that we could be called a son or daughter of encouragement. "If Christians would associate together, speaking to each other of the love of God and of the precious truths of redemption, their own hearts would be refreshed and they would refresh one another. We may be daily learning more of our heavenly Father, gaining a fresh experience of His grace … If we thought and talked more of Jesus, and less of self [or others], we should have more of His presence" (*Steps to Christ*, pp. 101, 102).

We are all looking for joy and peace, and God wants us to have it. As I look at my life and evaluate the times I was critical and judgmental, there was no real joy or peace. It was only when the Holy Spirit was able to get through this hard head of mine that the joy and peace was realized. I'm glad it's the responsibility of the Holy Spirit to transform us. It is not our job to take each other to task.

Chapter 11

What Happened to the Criticizers in the Bible?

You don't have to go far in Scripture to see what happened to those who criticized God or His people. Lucifer, who started the rebellion in heaven, has kept it going on earth, which has resulted in death and destruction. Here are just a few examples from the Word of God:

- Aaron and Miriam (Moses' brother and sister), Korah, Dathan, and Abiram (Num. 12, 16)
- The brothers of Joseph (Gen. 37–50)
- Haman (Esther)
- King Saul (1 Sam. 16–18)
- Those who sought Daniel's life (Dan. 6)
- Judas Iscariot (John 12:1–8)
- Prophets of Baal (1 Kings 18:37–40)
- The unforgiving servant in Jesus' parable (Matt. 18:23-35)

Most of the Scribes and Pharisees were also always criticizing and trying to trap Jesus. Their critical spirit finally drove them to institute a plan to kill the Son of God. Talk about the ultimate mistake that was fueled by criticism and hatred.

The early church was under constant scrutiny as is the church today, but unfortunately, a host of the put-downs today are coming from within the church family, and this should not be so. I don't know of any critical person who has ever brought anyone to Jesus, but I have seen people leave the church because that spirit so wounded their hearts.

When we look at the faithful servants of God who were criticized in biblical times, we see that they were highly favored by the Lord and rewarded for their level of integrity. Conversely, take a look at how the majority of the criticizers listed above received their just due. They and their families paid a severe penalty and will possibly be among the lost. However, I'm confident that the Lord will even judge them with great mercy. I'm glad that He is our Judge—our great and merciful Judge— yet He is also our great defense attorney.

This brings to mind an experience I was involved in. On a certain occasion before I became a Christian, I found myself on the wrong side of the law for a minor infraction. After spending a night locked up and on a hard bench, I was taken to the courthouse. While I waited for my name to be called, a person I knew also came in. I found out that he had a little more serious charge against him, and I inquired as to what he thought the judge would do to him. He said the judge would let him go. I was surprised to hear that and asked how he knew it. His response was, "The judge is my personal attorney." Needless to say, I watched with great interest as he was called to the bench. Sure enough, when he faced the judge, he was asked a few questions and then the charge against him was dismissed. I, on the other hand, had to pay a small fine before I could go home.

Bringing this illustration to a spiritual application, how will you stand before the judgment seat of God? Do you know the Judge and is He also your defense attorney? Or will you be criticizing Him too?

All of heaven is doing everything possible to save you. Nothing will be left undone; no stone left unturned. Everything that can be done will be done to save you. There will be no excuse for anyone who is lost. We have a Supreme Court in the United States. Their verdict is final, with no appeal. The judgment of the final royal Supreme Court of heaven will also have no appeal, but this verdict will be our eternal destiny. Jesus does not wish to keep anyone out of heaven—He longs for all to be saved. The gift if free, but we need to confess our sins and repent and allow Jesus to free us from all the baggage that is keeping us down. Then we can truly represent Jesus in our thoughts and actions. Remember, there will not be any faultfinding, criticism, gossiping, or any spirit contrary to Christ in heaven! Are you preparing for heaven by taking on Christ's character? I sure hope so, because that is what will guarantee us a place in heaven.

Chapter 12

United We Stand, Divided We Fall

Over the past thirty years I've noticed that those who are most frequently the targets of criticism are pastors, teachers, and conference officers. For some reason beyond my comprehension, the people in these positions are attacked most of the time without mercy. But this is the way the enemy wants it. Jude 8 states, "These dreamers defile the flesh, reject authority, and speak evil of dignitaries."

As it is stated in Scripture, Moses' criticizers thought they were doing God a service when in fact they were doing the service of the enemy. When we tear down our leaders, we are really no different than the people who rebelled against God and Moses. As Christians we are called to uplift and encourage rather than to find fault and destroy. How will we be able to stand before a holy God if we do not truly represent Him now in our lifetime on earth? How many will be found wanting? How many will realize that because of their pride and rebellious spirit they lost out on being with Jesus for eternity? "The Lord never blesses those who criticize and accuses their brethren, for this is Satan's work" (*Evangelism*, p. 102).

Pray for your conference officers, pastors, teachers, and local church leaders! If we are sincerely praying for them, we will not be looking for their faults but will be eager to help them and the ministry the Lord has placed in their hands. Just as the arms of Moses were supported and victory came, so it will be for us as we support the leaders of our church.

None of the conference officers, pastors, teachers, and local church leaders are perfect, but then again, neither are we! In the areas that they are not gifted in, help and support them. Encourage them! This statement sums things up nicely: "United we stand, divided we fall." Don't allow the enemy to use you to divide the family.

In the chapter titled "Christian Unity" in *Testimonies for the Church*, we read, "A house divided against itself cannot stand. When Christians contend, Satan comes in to take control" (vol. 5, p. 244). "Christians should regard it as a religious duty to repress a spirit of envy or emulation" (*Ibid.*, p. 242). "Difficulties are often caused by the venders of gossip, whose whispered hints and suggestions poison unsuspecting minds and separate the closest friends" (*Ibid.*, p. 241). "satan is constantly seeking to cause distrust, alienation, and malice among God's people" (*Ibid.*, p. 242).

I realize the above statements will cause some to dig in their heels and reply that we need to bring our leaders to accountability, but first let us reflect on our own accountability, and if there is any time left, we may have a split second to look at someone else. If there needs to be change in the leadership, Jesus will make the changes. We will not have to do it. Keep your focus on Jesus—He is the "author and finisher of our faith" (Heb. 12:2). The work is His. "He who has begun a good work in you will complete it until the day of Jesus Christ" (Phil. 1:6). "How careful should we be in every word and act to follow closely the Pattern, that our example may lead men to Christ" (*Testimonies for the Church*, vol. 5, p. 236).

Chapter 13
Blessed by a Spiritual Wife

The following very personal story, of which I am ashamed, is about forgiveness. I share it only to illustrate the power of God to heal and transform us. I also share it to bring glory to God and to my wife who, under the most difficult of circumstances, did not criticize but forgave. Some who knew me well referred to her as "the saint" or "the angel," and I have to agree. She was not only willing to go the extra mile but to go at least an extra hundred miles to keep the family together.

In 1979 I became a Christian. It was not through any type of hardship; it was only because of the grace of God. The Holy Spirit impressed me in an instant that I was heading in the wrong direction, and the Lord started leading me from where I was to where He wanted me to be. Before that and while married to my wife, I had a mistress for fifteen years. I virtually helped raise two families during this period of time. Why reveal this? Without going into any details, my wife realized this after the first year. However, she never once, during or after this affair, held this over my head. We have discussed the matter since, but she was very gracious and has never brought the subject up.

During this interracial affair the mistress conceived and bore a son. The Holy Spirit once again got through my hard heart, this time when the son of my mistress was twelve years old. My whole life changed in an instant. The Holy Spirit impressed me strongly that I was headed in the wrong direction. A 180-degree turnaround followed this impression. I asked my wife if we could start reading the Bible together, and she agreed. Praise God! At that time we had six children, ages nine to seventeen, and we all studied together.

But what about my other son? I could not just leave him, so I told my wife that I had another son and would like him to live with us. To my surprise, without hesitation, she said okay. Remember, she's an angel, and I wish I could have realized this years ago. We then told our other children, which was a very emotional experience for all of us. They were okay with the decision also. After asking his mother what she thought about the idea, she left the decision up to our son. He agreed to come and live with us, and for the next two years he stayed with us and everything went extremely well.

The first weekend he arrived we all adapted to having the newest member of the family with us. The bonding was instantaneous and went smoothly. On Sunday while I was getting something out of the closet, my wife came in and wrapped her arms around me and said, "I can see why you didn't want to leave him." Needless to say, my heart melted, and I thought, *Would I be so gracious if the situation were reversed?* Proverbs 31:26 says, "She opens her mouth with wisdom, and on her tongue is the law of kindness." How true!

Now, although the children are all grown, we still have a lot of family time together, and all the praise goes to our precious Lord and Savior, Jesus.

Some years later I asked his mother why and how she could let him stay with us. Even though she was under heavy pressure from her family not to let him do so (because they thought my wife would mistreat him), she said, "I know that you would not let him be mistreated, and I wanted him to know your side to the family." I then realized that the Lord blessed in spite of the terrible mistakes I had made in my life. How gracious and forgiving He is!

If you are going through a similar experience, I want to encourage you to hang in there. Pray and trust in the Lord. He will not only get you through this, but if you let Him, He will go through it with you. The Lord says, "I will never leave you nor forsake you" (Heb. 13:5). What a beautiful promise!

Let me also encourage those of you who are being criticized, especially if there is no just cause. The Lord is going through this with you. He experienced the same thing, even to a greater degree. Remain faithful to Him! To those whom the Holy Spirit is impressing to repent of your critical nature, change your direction before it's too late.

The book of James has some powerful admonitions for us. "If anyone among you thinks he is religious, and does not bridle his tongue but deceives his own heart, this one's religion is useless" (James 1:26). However, the Lord can change a useless religion into a useful one. James 3:8 states, "No man can tame the tongue. It is an unruly evil, full of deadly poison." Even though taming a critical tongue seems impossible "with God all things are possible" (Matt. 19:26).

Some of my favorite verses in the Bible are in 1 Peter 2, starting with verse 3: "If indeed you have tasted that the Lord is gracious. Coming to Him as a living stone, rejected indeed by men, but chosen by God and precious; you also, as living stones, are being built up a spiritual house, a holy priesthood, to offer up spiritual sacrifices acceptable to God through Jesus Christ" (verses 3–5). And Romans 12:1 tells us to "present your bodies a living sacrifice, holy, acceptable to God, which is your reasonable service."

In 1 Peter 2:9 we are reminded of our worth to God: "You are a chosen generation, a royal priesthood, a holy nation, His own special people, that you may proclaim the praises of Him who called you out of darkness into His marvelous light."

We are God's special people and as such our calling is high. We are children of the King—that makes us princes and princesses! Isn't it time for us to conduct ourselves for the honor and glory of our King, standing under the bloodstained banner of our Lord and Savior, Jesus? If we want to stand for Jesus, we have to be like Him—humble, meek, kind, and gentle. There is no place in the Christian's life for a critical spirit!! We are Christ's ambassadors and need to represent Him. It is your choice. Do you want to be a blessing or a curse to those around you? "Choose for yourselves this day whom you will serve ... but as for me and my house, we will serve the Lord" (Joshua 24:15).

About the Author

Jim Hammer has been involved in ministry for twenty-five years, serving as a lay pastor for approximately four years and head elder for more than twenty years. Through the course of his time in leadership he has witnessed the destruction of churches that entertain a critical spirit and the restoration of churches that adopt Christ's character. He hopes that readers will "search their hearts to see if they are building their church up or tearing it down." Now retired, his greatest joy comes from spending time with his wife, children, and grandchildren.

Jim is passionate about helping others develop a positive spirit and a Christlike character. A member of the New York Conference of Seventh-day Adventists, he has presented seminars at camp meeting, a prayer breakfast, and at various churches throughout the New York Conference.

He is available as a guest speaker and presenter for church seminars, camp meetings, and church and/or conference retreats. If you are interested in having Jim speak for an upcoming event, please contact him at 716-532-4099 or JHammer562@aol.com.

We invite you to view the complete
selection of titles we publish at:

www.TEACHServices.com

Scan with your mobile
device to go directly
to our website.

Please write or email us your praises, reactions, or
thoughts about this or any other book we publish at:

TEACH Services, Inc.
P U B L I S H I N G
www.TEACHServices.com

P.O. Box 954
Ringgold, GA 30736

info@TEACHServices.com

TEACH Services, Inc., titles may be purchased in bulk for
educational, business, fund-raising, or sales promotional use.
For information, please e-mail:

BulkSales@TEACHServices.com

Finally, if you are interested in seeing
your own book in print, please contact us at

publishing@TEACHServices.com

We would be happy to review your manuscript for free.

CPSIA information can be obtained at www.ICGtesting.com
Printed in the USA
LVOW080548241112

308627LV00002B/6/P